W9-ASC-268

DISCARD

The Library of Explorers and Exploration

PRINCE HENRY THE NAVIGATOR

Pioneer of Modern Exploration

Aileen Gallagher

the rosen publishing group's
rosen
central

For Sheila Affronti and Mike Gallagher,
my sister and brother, who always show me the way

Published in 2003 by The Rosen Publishing Group, Inc.
29 East 21st Street, New York, NY 10010

First Edition

Library of Congress Cataloging-in-Publication Data

Gallagher, Aileen.
Prince Henry the navigator : pioneer of modern exploration /
Aileen Gallagher.
    p. cm. — (The library of explorers and exploration)
Summary: Profiles Prince Henry of Portugal, whose support enabled explorers to claim new lands, spread Christianity, and increase trade between Europe and Africa while he, himself, remained close to home. Includes bibliographical references and index.
ISBN 0-8239-3621-X (lib. bdg.)
1. Henry, Infante of Portugal, 1394–1460—Juvenile literature.
2. Explorers—Portugal—Biography—Juvenile literature.
3. Princes—Portugal—Biography—Juvenile literature.
4. Geography, Medieval—Juvenile literature.
[1. Henry the Navigator, 1394–1460. 2. Explorers.]
I. Title. II. Series.
G286.H5 G35 2002
946.9'02'092—dc21
                                                2002003205

Manufactured in the United States of America

CONTENTS

INTRODUCTION

THE NAVIGATOR
WHO WASN'T

Prince Henry the Navigator, known in his native Portugal and throughout the world as a pioneer of exploration, never discovered new lands. Instead, Henry spent much of his life, from 1394 to 1460, at his home in Portugal. It was the sailors sent under his direction who witnessed new discoveries. But it was Henry who imagined that the world was larger than it appeared on the maps he read.

After gaining independence from Castile in 1385, the Portuguese kingdom was united for the next century. It faced no internal struggles for power and little threat of danger from neighboring countries. This period of peace allowed Portugal to concentrate its efforts on expanding territory and becoming a major power. Exploration, as it turned out, was the perfect way to meet both objectives.

Prince Henry the Navigator is largely considered the man responsible for Portugal's age of exploration. From 1419 until his death in 1460, he sent sailing expeditions down the west coast of Africa to break the Arab hold on trade routes and to establish colonies. Unfortunately, as a result of these expeditions, Portugal began a brutal slave trade that lasted for hundreds of years.

Prince Henry was part Portuguese and part English by birth. His English mother, Queen Philippa of Lancaster, instilled in him, and in all her children, the importance of their English ancestry and a sense of devotion to God. Philippa brought her family to the newly independent kingdom of Portugal. Henry, who according to the Portuguese chronicler Gomes Eanes de Zurara would later adopt the motto "a hunger to perform worthy deeds," did not disappoint his family or his kingdom.

Henry's first great achievement was in 1415. Along with the Portuguese army, led by his father King João I, he successfully attacked and conquered the North African city of Ceuta, which was then ruled by Moors (North African and Spanish Muslims).

Ceuta, which was also the center of the lucrative spice trade, was Henry's first attempt at a religious crusade. He saw it as his Christian duty to convert infidels, or nonbelievers, to his faith. His success against the Muslim city gave Henry an appetite for conquest, which would later prove disastrous.

Following its heyday as a world power during the fifteenth and sixteenth centuries, Portugal lost much of its wealth and status with the destruction of Lisbon in a 1755 earthquake, occupation during the Napoleonic Wars, and the 1822 independence of its colony Brazil. In 1974, a left-wing military takeover installed broad democratic reforms. The following year, Portugal granted independence to all of its African colonies, having given up its control of parts of India in 1961.

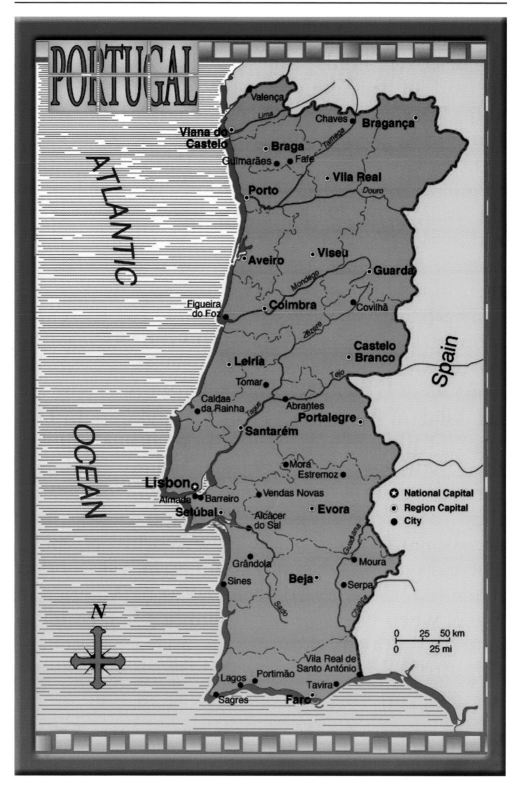

Besides spreading Christianity, Henry wanted to discover lands that lay beyond Portugal. Instead of traveling himself, however, he sent ships to explore Africa, where few white Europeans had ever been.

Before his sailors touched the shores of the mysterious continent, however, they happened upon the islands of Madeira and Porto Santo. As a result, the Portuguese settled both islands, which became valuable sources of natural resources for their kingdom.

The prince was also responsible for the enormous trading that began between Africa and Portugal in the fifteenth century. These expeditions were largely possible because of a particular kind of ship that Henry popularized. This vessel, called a caravel, could sail faster and farther than any other before it. Many explorers used these ships in the medieval world because they made traveling in the rough ocean—and accessing the fruits of the New World—possible. The caravel was actually among the vessels that made it across the Atlantic Ocean to America in 1492, when Christopher Columbus helped navigate two caravels and one nao, a larger merchant ship, from European shores.

Prince Henry also played an important role in the slave trade. Though buying and selling slaves was not new when Portugal entered into the business in the 1440s, slavery was not nearly as widespread as Henry would help it become. Henry's ships, besides trading goods, also kidnapped people from Africa and brought them to Portugal, where they would later be sold throughout Europe. When the prince helped sailors reach Africa, the slave trade flourished.

But Prince Henry's legacy would not be solidified in his individual acts. Because he dared to dream and had the determination to confirm that the world was bigger than previously believed, his legend became one that would help shape what historians would later call the age of exploration.

1

LAND'S END

If Spain is the head of Europe, Portugal, where land ends and sea begins, is the crown upon the head.
—Excerpt from the epic poem *Os Lusiadas* (The Lusiads) by Luís de Camões, 1572

Prince Henry, later known as the Navigator, was a major contributor to Portugal's advancements during the Renaissance. In fact, during his later years, Prince Henry was Portugal's maritime hero, with most of Europe's most renowned navigators, mapmakers, and shipbuilders rushing to his service. High upon a promontory (a high point of land that extends over a body of water), he was known to analyze maps and nautical charts from the world over. His castle upon that rock—Portugal's "Land's End"—was, as legend reported, located near Cape St. Vincent on Sagres Point on Cabo San

Modern historians doubt that Prince Henry founded a school of navigation at Sagres Point, as this illustration suggests. They do believe that the site may have been home to a fifteenth-century astrological observatory, a library that housed books of nautical charts called portolans, a chapel, and a wind rose, a structure still visible on Sagres's grounds. Archaeologists think the wind rose was used to determine wind speed and direction.

Vincenzo. Although legend also states that he built a school of navigation there, calling upon the era's most creative mapmakers and mathematicians to help him discuss the sea's potential, there is no evidence of its existence. Historians now believe that the legendary school was some kind of "seaman's hall," where information and ideas were shared. Unfortunately, unlike his brothers, Henry wrote no books that have survived to tell his story accurately.

Portugal was pushed into the forefront of the exploration age partly because of its location. Situated on the Iberian Peninsula, it faced the Atlantic Ocean, not the Mediterranean Sea. Portugal also had navigable rivers that led easily out to the ocean. But fourteenth-century Portugal was isolated from the rest of Europe. Its explorers knew little about the lands west of the country and even less about the mysterious continent to the south known as Africa.

Prior to the Renaissance, and the paths imagined by Portugal's prized prince, discovery of new lands was mostly accidental. Knowledge of foreign lands was gained only when ships were misguided by winds or lost at sea. The sailors who did return would tell stories of their journeys, but most of those accounts were never written down. Sailors were not highly educated people; very few of them could read well. Sometimes, accounts of the voyages were kept secret because merchants wanted to protect their trading routes and profits.

This is a Spanish nautical map of western Europe from 1592. The thin projections radiating out from certain points are called rhumb lines. They were included on maps of the era to show navigators the most direct courses for sailing.

Yet another great obstacle faced by early explorers was the inaccuracy of available maps. Before there were proper maps, sailors relied only on nautical charts. These charts were later included in books called *portolans*, which is Italian for "pilot book." The portolans, which mostly originated from Italian cities like Genoa, contained information about ports, coastlines, and harbors. The portolans, in fact, were still in use as late as 1595 by Dutch mariners, the best seamen of the day. Still, the portolans provided information only about the coasts, not the open sea. Explorers knew almost nothing about the ocean and even less about the land around which the sea moved.

Cartography in the Middle Ages

Theologians, or religious scholars, drew some of the earliest maps. Theologians were the most educated people of their time. To create maps, they used the Bible as a guide. Because biblical interpretations were repeated over time, maps contained the same mistakes for hundreds of years. Only sailors who physically explored the lands and surrounding seas could offer correct interpretations of those maps. However, thirteenth-century Portuguese sailors typically explored only the shallow waters that bordered the continents, such as along the Mediterranean Sea, and then only about

In the Middle Ages, people were fearful of the unknown, commonly describing natural phenomena that did not exist. Sea monsters were no exception. This illustration might depict a serpent known as an Orchun.

500 miles north and south of Portugal. Sailors faithfully followed the coastline on their voyages, never venturing into the ocean's depths, which were still unknown and mysterious.

Maps in 1394, when Prince Henry was born, showed not only what people had actually seen but also what mapmakers, explorers, and leading thinkers of the time believed was there. Entire sections of world maps were labeled as unknown territory. Horrific stories circulated among even the most educated men about the condition of the open sea. Sailors told tales of lost

Mapping the Unknown

Throughout Europe's medieval world, Christians murdered Jews because of their religious beliefs. Because Jews had been persecuted for centuries, they were forced to become a nomadic people always searching for new refuge and safety. They had also drawn maps during their frequent traveling and offered them to kings who gave them safe haven. But the Judaic maps were much different than those drawn by Christian scholars, and not only because they were more accurate. Christians drew complete maps by filling in areas no one had seen with lands drawn from the Bible and mythology. The Jewish maps dared to leave areas blank, with great expanses of land marked unknown. The maps drawn by Jews were far more enticing to explorers than the Christian maps, which warned sailors of giant beasts and hostile people.

A Jew named Abraham Cresques drew the best surviving map of the period in 1375 for the king of Aragon. Though there is little evidence to support it, Portuguese legend has it that Abraham's son, Yehuda, took his mapmaking skills to Portugal in the fifteenth century.

ships and huge sea monsters that threatened vessels once they ventured too far from the familiar coastline. Others were convinced that human skin would turn black if exposed to what they believed were direct rays from the sun nearest the equator. People also thought the ocean water boiled near the Tropics, and these waters were sometimes referred to as seas of blood.

Europe and Asia commonly formed the top section of most maps, with the eastern coast of Africa adjacent to Europe. The African continent was normally shown as a cropped land mass because its eastern coast was part of what was considered unknown territory. An unnamed continent remained constant at the bottom section, too, because if there was no land there, the earth would be unbalanced. Most uneducated Europeans in 1394 thought the world was flat.

Portugal had a geographical advantage in that it was physically close to the African continent; for years, the Portuguese had traded with Muslim merchants from northern Africa. Portugal was also a land of many different nationalities and had been settled by Celts, Iberians, and Englishmen, all of whom influenced its culture. Though Christianity was by far the major religion of Portugal, Jews and Muslims lived there, too. The Portuguese had even intermarried with Asians and Africans. Portugal's diversity became a source of strength for its kingdom.

Before the Portuguese discovered they could sail around the Cape of Good Hope, Muslim traders crossed hundreds of miles of desert in caravans to deliver their goods to European markets. The journeys were often brutal and cost many traders their lives. Being able to instead sail around Africa made trade and transportation safer, easier, and less costly.

Prince Henry was responsible for what is called a paradigm shift in thinking. A paradigm is a model or pattern. A paradigm shift occurs when the old patterns are destroyed with creative thinking and new ideas.

For example, the pattern of trade from Africa in the early part of the fifteenth century was consistent: Moors, or Muslims, would trade with native people on the western coast of Africa. The Muslims would then trek east across the desert in caravans to port cities in the northeast, accessible by European merchants. The paradigm shift occurred when the caravan was eliminated—when European ships could go to the west coast to trade with the merchants themselves. Prince Henry was responsible for many paradigm shifts, all of which changed the course of history.

PROPHECY AND PROFIT

He is bound to engage in great and noble conquests, and above all to attempt the discovery of all things which were hidden from other men and secret.

—Gomes Eanes de Zurara, 1394

At the time of Prince Henry's birth in 1394, Portuguese life was difficult, but exploration was already under way. For curious seamen, the shores of Africa represented danger, but they also meant the possibility of great riches. Travel was a challenge, so people were forced to survive only on available materials. Exploration and trade allowed people to acquire goods from other places.

Meat and poultry, pictured in this depiction of a sixteenth-century kitchen of nobility, were the staple foods of the wealthy. Europeans, however, lacked spices, so trade in spices from the East was a lucrative business. During the Middle Ages, a pound of ginger was worth the price of a sheep, a pound of mace would buy three sheep or half a cow, and cloves cost the equivalent of about $20 a pound. Pepper, always the greatest prize, was counted out peppercorn by peppercorn.

This is an eighteenth-century French print of a nutmeg plant, one of the most prized spices in medieval trade. By the seventeenth century, the Dutch ruled the market with an iron fist. They soaked their nutmeg in milk of lime, a process that did not affect their flavor but supposedly killed the seed of the nut. This was to prevent nutmeg from being planted elsewhere.

Food and its preparation had much to do with these developments. Wealthy people ate a great deal of meat, but it quickly went bad in Portugal's warm climate. The only way to preserve meat or fish was to smoke it or salt it, which sometimes worsened its taste. Spices such as nutmeg improved the flavor of food, or at least covered up its rotting smell. In fact, nutmeg was so precious that during the fifteenth and sixteenth centuries it was sometimes used in place of currency.

Spices were expensive because they were so difficult to obtain. Merchants, traveling on foot, normally took several months to trek over African deserts with foreign goods like spices, textiles, silks, and precious stones and metals. In fact, merchants were so often exposed to such rigorous traveling that it was never surprising if they didn't return at all. Some were lost to foul weather, others were lost to disease. And in every such case, the people who paid for the journey lost money. As a result, it was only the countries that had regular access to spices and other desirable goods that became wealthy.

Muslims embraced a much different religion and culture than the Europeans, who were mostly Christian. The Muslims controlled access to India, which was the heart of the spice trade. Between 1096 and 1291, Europeans had tried to forcibly convert Muslims to Christianity in campaigns called the Crusades. Christians, who felt morally obligated to spread their faith, repeatedly tried to capture the Holy Land from the Muslims.

Favorite Son

Prince Henry, also known as the Infante Dom Henrique, was the third surviving son of João I (John) and Philippa of Lancaster. He was born on March 4, 1394. Philippa was

from England, then one of the world's most powerful kingdoms. A daughter of the duke and duchess of Lancaster, Philippa belonged to England's royal family. Although it was said that Henry was one of his father's favorite sons, his mother's influence would have an even greater impact on his life.

Because most royalty throughout Europe looked to the stars as well as the church for guidance, Prince Henry's astrological chart was written for him on the day of his birth. This was not unusual, as most royal families recorded this same type of birth information.

Gomes Eanes de Zurara, Portugal's keeper of the national archives, recalled this chart in detail. Zurara was what was known as a chronicler or scribe, one whose job it was to write and keep the history of royalty.

In his *Chronicle of the Capture of Ceuta* and *Chronicle of the Discovery and Conquest of Guinea*, Zurara told the story of Portugal's important role in the age of exploration. However, because Henry was a member of the royal court, it was his intention to tell his story in as positive a light as possible, making historians somewhat critical of his writing.

In Renaissance Portugal, astrology was taken as seriously as any other field of study. Juan Ruiz, a fourteenth-century Spanish writer, gave weight to star charts when he wrote, "In the science of astrology, a worthy

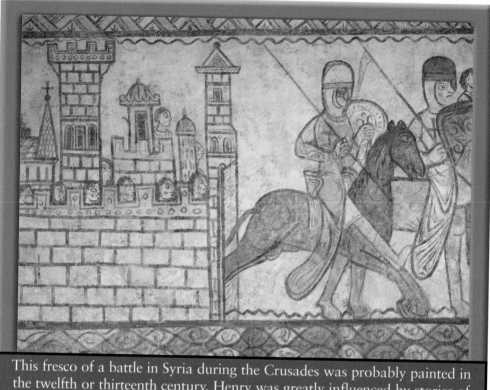

This fresco of a battle in Syria during the Crusades was probably painted in the twelfth or thirteenth century. Henry was greatly influenced by stories of the Crusades, and at a young age he was inducted into the Order of Christ, a Portuguese military order of monks devoted to spreading Christianity and regaining the Holy Land of Jerusalem from the Muslims.

branch of learning, the astrologers of old declare that, when a man is born, they take the sign that is dominant at the moment of his birth to lay down the path his life will take." In his *Chronicle of the Discovery and Conquest of Guinea*, Zurara wrote that the stars predestined Henry for "great and noble conquests and to the uncovering of secrets previously hidden from men." For a man who would be remembered by history as "the Navigator," his horoscope would be frequently recalled by friends and family members during Henry's life.

Portugal was politically independent during Henry's lifetime, after years of political strife with Castile, a kingdom in Spain and Portugal's eastern neighbor on the southwest coast of Europe. The war had cost Portugal quite a bit of money, making increased trade, and the resulting profits, more important than ever.

Although the Crusades were long over with by the time he was born, Prince Henry, a devout Catholic, still believed it was important to convert Muslims to Christianity. Henry's entire family was very pious (religious). They took their religion so seriously, in fact, that they funded a theology program at Lisbon University. Henry felt it was the duty of every Christian to save pagans by converting them to Christianity. But, as a person of royalty and privilege, he felt even more aligned with this responsibility. This meant finding new parts of the world in which to spread his faith.

A Privileged Life

Although few facts of his youth were recorded, it is known that Henry was educated by his mother in his home in Oporto. From a young age, Henry knew the tales of his ancestry and had a strong sense of chivalry from his mother's English heritage. She impressed upon her sons their noble background and its royal significance. Still, the role of royalty was

IOANNES I. LVSITANIÆ REX X.

King João I of Portugal *(above)* made his son, Afonso, the duke of Bragança (also called Braganza) in 1442. Afonso's descendants became the wealthiest noble landowners in Portugal. The royal house of Bragança ruled Portugal from 1640 to 1910, and Brazil from 1822 to 1889.

changing at the dawn of the fifteenth century, and some monarchs who were once considered harsh dictators were now benevolent father figures, called by God to guide their subjects. Royalty now had a divine duty to care for the people. Henry's father, King João I, chose a new banner to symbolize his duty. On it, a camel carried four sacks, each of which had a motto written upon it: "Fear an unwise rule," "Judge justly," "Console the afflicted," and "Accomplish great deeds with economy."

From his parents, Henry learned the power of nobility and the responsibilities that came with the title of prince, such as learning the tactics of warfare and diplomacy. He also enjoyed living in grand style, as befitted nobility. He loved lavish clothing and exquisite food. His sense of pageantry meant that everything around him had to be the best.

Prince Henry received his first large gift when he was fourteen years old. His father, the king, gave each of his three oldest sons their own plots of land. Since Portugal was a small and relatively poor country, the king couldn't give his sons all the land he wanted, but their estates grew over time. By 1411, Henry received his first house. The estate was in a hilly part of northern central Portugal called Viseu. Though there are no detailed descriptions of the property, the original deed described a medieval country estate with twenty-three small houses surrounding the larger main living quarters.

With the estate came increased responsibility. To help his sons learn about leadership, the king put them on the state council as his advisers. Henry learned more about the world around him. His position of influence with his father made it possible to organize voyages. Henry and his brothers convinced their father of the benefits of exploration, including the riches that were likely to be found in Africa. Their insistence got them further than anyone had imagined. By the end of the 1400s, Portugal was a world power.

3

THE FIRST CRUSADE

Many reliable historians have written about the knightly deeds of arms and about the tales of valor performed by many kings, dukes, and princes, but it is certain that in none of these writings will be found another example of the seizure by force of arms in so short a time of such a large and famous city.
—Zurara, *Chronicle of the Capture of Ceuta*, 1415

Ships left the Portuguese port of Tagus frequently, but the morning of July 26, 1415, was different. Portugal, despite its financial hardships, was about to make history. The royal family, with Prince Henry's help, had assembled the largest naval fleet ever collected in the country's history and set sail on a southward course. A Castilian spy named Ruy Diaz de Vega reported to King Fernando of Aragon that the army had 19,000 men on this historic and secret mission. However, except for the Portuguese royal family and the fleet's high command, no one knew where they were going.

PRINCE HENRY
OF
PORTUGAIL

HONI SOIT QVI MAL Y PENSE

CEUTA

The Invasion of Ceuta

Their destination was a small city named Ceuta, 160 miles southeast of the Portuguese mainland, in North Africa. The land belonged to Morocco, a Muslim kingdom. It was a busy and wealthy port, as well as one of the strongest forces in the Mediterranean Sea. As a commercial trading center, Ceuta was the point of export for large quantities of wheat. Because it was situated between Europe and Africa, Ceuta served as a doorway to both African gold and European silver.

Although Morocco controlled the city of Ceuta, people of all faiths worked and lived there peacefully. Christian traders did business among Muslims without hesitation and freely practiced their religion. For generations, people of various and diverse cultures prospered there.

But Prince Henry told his people a very different story. In Zurara's *Chronicle of the Capture of Ceuta*, the prince's biographer paints an elaborate picture, as told to him by Henry. The ships set sail that morning to seize Ceuta and force its citizens to convert to Christianity. For the Portuguese, this was a crusade. For the young men who volunteered for the adventure, it was a chance to prove themselves in battle as their fathers had done against Spain.

Prince Henry is shown in full battle regalia in this rare engraving. Henry participated in the Battle of Ceuta as an armed knight. He fought with such valor that his father, João I, king of Portugal, named him the duke of Viseu. In 1418, he settled at Sagres, where he often met with navigators and scholars.

As Zurara wrote, King João had suggested an international tournament to celebrate peace with Castile and the knighting of his three oldest sons in 1411. The princes, Duarte, Pedro, and Henry, wanted more than jousting tournaments and games. The young princes wanted to celebrate Portugal's new status as an independent nation by spreading its influence and increasing its wealth and power.

King João was hesitant. If an attack on Ceuta were to be successful, it would have to be kept secret for as long as possible. But in order to gather ships and men for the mission, the country's merchant class would have to contribute to its cause. This was unlikely, especially since the nature of their investment would have to remain a secret. The proposed attack posed other threats: The Muslim countries of northern Africa would be likely to strike back, and the government of Castile, which considered Ceuta a city within a region it controlled, might also grow angry at Portugal's decision to strike.

But Henry fervently led his brothers and patiently struck down every argument made by their father. God was on their side, Henry explained. Because they were spreading Christianity, God would grant Portugal's army success and protection. Still, the king doubted his sons' agenda. He was unsure if he had the legal and moral right to invade a land that posed no threat to him, his

Ceuta is located on a promontory on the coast of North Africa, as shown in this seventeenth-century map by Pietro de Cortona. In the medieval period, it was the hub of the spice trade, with goods arriving from the East before being sent on to European markets. This led the Portuguese to annex it in 1415. It was re-won by the Arabs, who later lost it to the Spanish, who still control it to this day.

This sixteenth-century hand-colored woodcut depicts Lisbon, the capital of Portugal. Rich in detail, the engraving shows the city's fortifications and the armada of ships in its harbor. Life inside the city walls, however, was marked by cramped, unsanitary living conditions, making it a prime target for the bubonic plague epidemics that swept through Europe from the fourteenth to sixteenth centuries.

people, or their right to practice Christianity. The king spoke to priests, lawyers, merchants, and scholars. They assured him that the invasion would be "in God's service."

With these blessings and loans from Portuguese merchants, King João I gave his permission to sail. Prince Henry could now lead the army to Ceuta.

In gathering his force, Henry spared no amount of pageantry. The army and navy gathered in Lisbon, Portugal's later-named capital. Its military leaders were dressed in rich

colors and sailed on ships that flew brightly colored flags and banners. Despite Portugal's financial strife, its military would look just as grand as Europe's greatest armies. To Prince Henry, it was a chance to call attention to his country's greatness, for he was the leader of the showy army.

Dire Portents

The plague, a deadly disease of the Middle Ages, was a great danger throughout Europe for hundreds of years. Portuguese cities, such as Lisbon, were very unsanitary. Shortly before Henry's fleet put to sea, his mother contracted the disease. Queen Philippa died from the plague on July 15. According to leg-

This drawing of a solar eclipse was published in 1724 in *Parker's London News*. Eclipses, both solar and lunar, are believed by many world religions to have some supernatural significance.

end, Philippa remained alive long enough to give her three sons new swords to bless them on their historic journey. Just hours later, she was dead. That same night, there was a solar eclipse. Events of ill omen had cast doubts on the expedition.

Members of João's court soon suggested that the expedition be delayed for more than a month. It would take at least that long for proper funeral ceremonies. But the princes would have none of it and instead pressed the importance of their trip to their father. In response, the king shortened the official period of mourning to just a week, a shockingly short time for the death of a royal. The princes and their fleet set sail on July 26, just eight days after the queen's death.

The omens, although natural in occurrence, seemed to have troubled the mission from its beginning. The Portuguese fleet was in danger from the start. The lack of wind in eerily calm waters caused the ships to sit listlessly in the sea. The fleet didn't even make it into the Strait of Gibraltar—only about 250 miles southeast of Lisbon—until August 10. The strait was difficult to navigate, and it proved too ambitious for several of the Portuguese captains. The fleet was split as a result. The royal galleons commanded by King João eventually made it to the northern side of Ceuta. Meanwhile, the merchant ships, holding the soldiers commanded by Prince Pedro, were forced by the mighty wind toward Malaga, the province of Granada's main port. King João could only sit off the coast of Ceuta and wait for his son and his ships to return. The mistake cost the Portuguese the all-important element of surprise.

A Change in Strategy

In response, the governor of Ceuta, Salah ben Salah, quickly called for reinforcements from the Moroccan mainland. There was plenty of time for him to reinforce the city since it took another two days for the Portuguese ships to rejoin the royal galleons. King João, who had anchored farther south than originally planned, took an opportunity to refocus the battle plan.

Ceuta was built on seven hills. The port city was strong and protected, but its highest elevations were another matter. While the king waited for Pedro's ship, he decided an attack on the well-fortified Monte Almina would be a better plan. Although the Portuguese knew little about naval warfare, they were excellent foot soldiers and had learned much about strategy from years of fighting with Spain.

The new plan could not be put into action immediately, however. As soon as Prince Pedro's ships arrived and anchored with his father's, a violent storm blew up. The ships returned to waters off Castile and anchored there instead. King João and his advisers walked along the Castilian shoreline and debated what to do next. Many thought the plan should be abandoned and that the fleet should return to Portugal. The plague from Lisbon had made its way onto the ships. Other soldiers, not accustomed to sailing, were weak from seasickness. Zurara wrote that the

three princes again urged their father to reconsider the conquest. But Duarte, writing later, said King João decided to continue. This made sense, too, because the king was pressured. Leading an army to retreat before an attack would be incredibly embarrassing, possibly damaging his relationships with other European monarchs.

King João and his inexperienced fleet conquered Ceuta on August 21, 1415, in one day. In all, only eight men in Henry's army were lost in the battle.

The victory was possible because of a number of factors, not all of them related to the skills of the Portuguese army. Because there was no Moroccan navy to challenge the Portuguese fleet, the king and his ships could maneuver at will, with the weather presenting their only challenge. Foolishly, Governor ben Salah had sent his reinforcements back to the mainland as soon as he saw the Portuguese fleet leave the waters around Ceuta a week earlier. Moreover, the city, like the rest of Morocco, was struck by famine and plague, weakening the few forces that fought. When ben Salah decided that the Portuguese were a threat, he ordered his troops from the fort on Monte Almina to attack the king's men who were coming ashore. But he failed to guess that King João had decided to take the fort first, and then the city.

In an eyewitness account of the battle sent to Fernando of Aragon, it seemed that the Portuguese used their cannons, though

Zurara made no mention of the Portuguese bombarding Ceuta. But an eyewitness account found in a collection of primary source material called the *Monumenta Henricina* tells a different story: "After attacking the city with a great number of bombards and other artillery, the place was captured in the space of thirteen hours." Zurara's *Chronicle of the Capture of Ceuta* continued, saying that Prince Henry asked his father to be the first man ashore, but that honor went instead to Prince Duarte, the heir to the Portuguese throne.

Prince Henry's actions on that day were brave indeed. But Henry was dangerous to himself and to others. The prince rushed ahead of his men and found himself alone on a side street, surrounded by the enemy. Henry, at twenty-one years of age, was a large, strong man, but his size made him perhaps more daring than he should have been. He likely would have died at the hands of the Moroccans had not the governor of his household at Viseu, a friend and mentor, come to save him. Unfortunately, the rescue cost the governor his life.

Knightly Honors

After the Portuguese had control of Ceuta, they set about plundering it, taking its beautiful tapestries, exotic silks, and luxurious gems. The soldiers knew there was gold in Ceuta and immediately set out to find it. Unfortunately, they

Muslims stand inside the inner sanctuary of a mosque in North Africa. This woodcut from the eighteenth century reproduces the architectural details of a traditional mosque, including the arches, the tile and inlay work on the walls, and the typical handblown glass lamp hanging from the ceiling.

destroyed most of the valuable spices and oils in their search. But few of the Portuguese commanders cared. Zurara wrote, "This destruction caused much wailing among some of those of lowly origin but respectable and noble persons did not trouble themselves about such things."

After the looting, the Portuguese considered the religious nature of their quest. They went to Ceuta's mosques, the Muslim houses of worship, and blessed them as Christian churches. King João gathered his three sons in a church, now called Santa Maria da Misericórdia, and knighted each of them. In the ceremony, he used the swords presented to his sons by their mother, the late Queen Philippa. He then annexed Ceuta for the kingdom of Portugal.

The king was so impressed with Henry's actions on Ceuta, in fact, that he allowed his son to conduct the ceremony of turning over its keys to the new Portuguese governor, Pedro de Meneses.

De Meneses had the trust and confidence of both King João and his sons. Before setting sail for the return to Portugal in September, the king ordered Prince Henry to instruct the governor on how to best defend the city. It is doubtful that the twenty-one-year-old prince, fresh from his first battle, had much valuable information. For the moment, however, Henry must have felt like king of the world.

4

UNSEEN LANDS

*Little by little was exiled our sight, from hills of our own land
that lay behind . . . Until at length all vanished utterly, And we
saw nothing but the sky and the sea. Thus we went forth to break
those oceans through, Where none before had ever forced the way.*
—Excerpt from the epic poem *Os Lusiadas*
(The Lusiads) by Luís de Camões, 1572

P rince Henry spent the next several years actively
involved with the affairs of Ceuta. On February
18, 1416, King João appointed him controller
of "all matters pertaining to our city of Ceuta and
the defense thereof," as it was recorded in the
Monumenta Henricina. This was meant as a gesture
to his son, who had wanted to be the governor of
Ceuta himself. In his appointment, the king never
bothered, perhaps on purpose, to distinguish any
difference between Henry's new role and that of
Governor de Meneses. But the two men remained
friendly, with de Meneses even loaning the prince
sums of money.

Prince Henry commissioned this world map by Fra Mauro of Venice, Italy.
Henry required Portuguese explorers to keep logs of their voyages to aid the
Arab, Italian, German, and Scandinavian cartographers with whom he shared
information. Their research led to developments in navigational instruments
such as the quadrant and new tables to aid in determining latitude.

Austen

Oceanus

Mare Indicum

Siroco

Mare Indicum

Saylan

Mare Indicum

Peligondi

Deli

India
Seconda

Phison

Tibet

Cina

Serica

Tanqui

Lop

Deserto

Zouza

Chatajo

Chatajo

Xandu

M. Altai

Diab

Soffala

Diab   Xengibar

Chancibar

I. Diviamoal

I. Diu

Cholecut

Gutzrat

Mare Persicum

Oriza

Bisenegal   Soltanfur

Deserto

Thate

Persia
Chobinam

Madegan   Cremania
Lago

Media

Babilonia
Caldea

Persia

Tigris

Assiria

Balach

Armenia

Archa
Noe

Chorasia Sirax

Here   Spahan   Thauris

Mare Breunto   Tharse   Soltania   Tiphis

P. Sace   Mar Chaspio

Deserto   Balch
P. Jerchan   Fl. Mur

Paglu di
fero

Insical   Organza
Samargant

P. Gothan   Sarey

Fl. Edil

Silua   Rossia Negra
Tangut

Mar   Nairat   Rossia Biaheda
Biancha   P. Destini

Dislana   P. Nef

P. Sibir   P. Balimata

Sepolero   P. Meschiera
Incam   M. Iperborei   P. Cestan

Permia

Septem

Tramontana

Etiopia
Australe

Fl. Galla

Fl. Zebe

Ethyopia

Ziada   Barara   Etiopia Occidentale
Saba   R. Gogian
Fl. Azasi   Ilamara
P. Fataor
P. Davaro Bagamidri   Fonte
Nadaber   Geneth   Gozan
Abafsin   Fl. Abavi

Adel   Beniclelb

Ifat   Fl. Tigai

Zilla   Deuchali

Aden   Merve Palude
Arabia
Felice   Mergi Melli
Mecha

Thasi   Arabia   Nuba
Arabia
Suin

Susiana   Deserta   Sayto
Deserto

Judea   Egypto   Egypto Libia   Cirenaica

Siria   Mare Mediterraneum

Damasco

Asia minor

Monte Thauro   Macedonia

Pontus Euxinus   Servia
Bolgaria   Alemagna
Zorania   Danubio
Ungaria

Tartaria   Polana   Pragu
Prusia

Fl. Tanai

Rossia Rossia

Lituana   Riga

Alana   Rossia
Noagra   Novograd

Moschovia   Rossia   Filandia

Cigarchia
Inferior   Cavo di
Rossia
Permia

Alt. piedi parig. 5, poll. 11, lin. 7.

Governor of the Order of Christ

After several years of helping to lead Ceuta, Henry received an even greater honor. On May 25, 1420, the pope, the leader of the Catholic Church, appointed Henry the administrator general, or governor, of the Order of Christ. This military group was told to "defend the Faith," or help to lead crusades in the lands of the infidels and convert them to Christianity. It was under the Order of Christ that Henry would lead future quests.

For Henry, the appointment meant great prestige and power. The Order was wealthy, as it kept much of the money and valuables that it stole from foreign lands, and Henry later admitted that the Order financed many of Portugal's journeys of exploration.

As an administrator, Henry was not a member of the Order, though he was later invited to join the group. And although he never took the vows of celibacy (abstaining from sexual relations) and poverty that the Order required, his own lifestyle reflected similar values. Many historians, in fact, compare his lifestyle to that of a monk. Prince Henry, an educated man who collected maps and books, never married and had no children, and likely was celibate his entire life.

In the early 1420s, Henry seemed content to lead the Order of Christ and monitor the affairs of Ceuta. But by 1424, he had another goal: He wanted to increase Portugal's wealth and power by finding lands to colonize and farm. The groups of islands that he had in mind were situated off the west coast of Morocco and the Sahara desert. One of the island chains, or archipelagoes, was called the Canary Islands. Another was a small group of islands, the largest of which was called Madeira. The archipelagoes were in the Atlantic Ocean, which was referred to on maps of the time as the Ocean Sea because many fifteenth-century mapmakers believed that all waters of the world were one. In fact, so little was known about geography that many of the islands on maps were later found not to exist at all.

While most European kings had maps, Prince Henry was the first to actually compare the information on the maps to what explorers and mariners had seen for themselves. The prince sent explorers out to sea to confirm geographical information. Henry's connection with the Portuguese Order of Christ gave him the money he needed to mount the expensive expeditions that began regularly in 1424. For the young prince, it was a fine chance to bring himself greater glory, claim new lands for Christianity, and bring wealth to the kingdom of Portugal by establishing trade relationships with other kingdoms.

Slave trading became a major commercial enterprise after Portuguese explorations of the African west coast. This illustration of a group of slaves on board a slave ship is taken from the *Illustrated London News*, June 20, 1857.

From Exploration to Exploitation

In 1424, Henry gathered a large army of several thousand mounted and foot soldiers. The governor of his household at Viseu, Fernando de Castro, commanded the army. Supporting, training, and leading an army of this size was an expensive prospect. In order to gain the support he needed, Henry claimed that his purpose was to convert the large pagan population who lived on the Canaries to Christianity. But, as time went

on, attempts at conversion on African soil gave way to kidnapping and, eventually, active Portuguese participation in the slave trade.

His first attempt, in 1424, was an utter failure. It was so humiliating for Portugal, and for the prince, that barely any account of the battle exists. In his chronicle, Zurara recalled the event with one sentence only: "He also sent a very large expedition against the Canary Islands for the purpose of showing [the people] there the road to our holy faith." The native people, a group much stronger than Henry ever anticipated, drove the crusading Christians back to Portugal. But defeat did not stop Henry's desire for glory and wealth. He instead turned his eye toward the island of Madeira, about 300 miles north of the Canary Islands.

Madeira had appeared on maps and seamen's charts since 1351, though two of Henry's squires claimed to have "discovered" it in 1425, when they were blown off course during a storm. The two men, John Gonçalves Zarco and Tristão Vaz, claimed that the islands of Madeira and Porto Santo, a smaller island twenty-eight miles to the northeast, were perfect for colonization. King João ordered the two men to prepare for their voyage for the purposes of colonizing the islands. In doing so, they led a group of colonists to claim them as a royal territory of Portugal.

Madeira and Porto Santo

The word *madeira* means "wood" in the Portuguese language. The term accurately described the island, since its 286 square miles were covered with a dense forest. Although both of the islands were without any signs of human life, the surrounding waters teemed with fish. The colonists could live off these fish on Porto Santo while harvesting the timber on Madeira. And because wood was a scarce natural resource in Portugal, Madeira would be an important new colony.

There were no animals of any kind on Porto Santo, so the settlers, possibly at Henry's suggestion, brought rabbits there as a source of meat for the workers. This was a terrible idea. The rabbits soon multiplied and overran the island, eating its grasses and any available vegetables. The rabbits made it impossible to grow anything, so instead the colonists raised cattle, fished, and exported "dragon's blood," a resin from the dragon tree that was used to dye clothes at the time.

This nineteenth-century drawing combines an illustration of a dragon tree with the island on which it is most commonly found, the island of Madeira in the Atlantic Ocean. The red liquid obtained from the dragon tree was used to dye clothes and was also believed to cure dysentery.

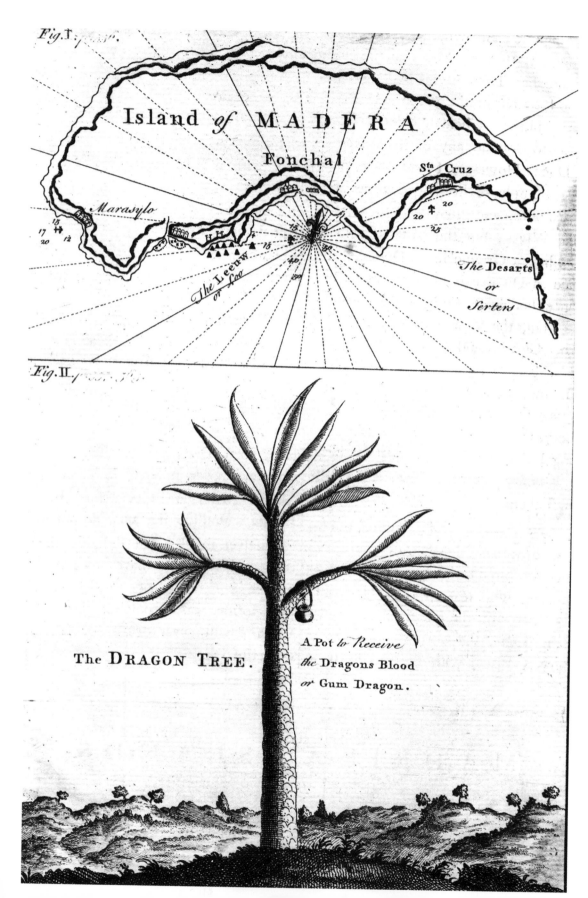

Fig.I. *p.76.*

Island *of* MADERA

Fonchal

Sta Cruz

Marasylo

The Leeuw or Loo

The Desarts or Serters

Fig.II. *p.76. Fig.*

The DRAGON TREE.

A Pot to Receive
the Dragons Blood
or Gum Dragon.

Henry left a Genoese named Bartolomeo Pallastrelli, who had settled in Portugal at the end of the fourteenth century, in charge of the struggling colony. Pallastrelli, a knight of Henry's household of Viseu, would later become the father-in-law of an explorer named Christopher Columbus.

The island of Madeira was a colonial success story. Except for a fire that threatened part of it (the settlers had tried burning down some trees as a way to clear land), the colony thrived. Fresh water was plentiful. The soil, rich after hundreds of years of dead leaves fertilizing it, guaranteed hearty crops. Grapes grew especially well in Madeira, and the island gave name to a famous type of sweet wine as a result.

Madeira's success was not only meaningful to Portugal but also to Henry's personal reputation. Again he had gone with his instincts, ignoring those who said the voyage could not be made. The naysayers in Portugal who simply found Henry to be a religious zealot with an urge to start expensive wars with Muslims were finally proven wrong. Henry brought his country profit as well as glory. Yet publicly, Henry pledged that his only motivation was his desire to convert pagans and infidels to Christianity. He claimed that the attempted settlement of the Canary

Islands was part of his crusade against Islam. He even told Pope Eugenius IV that he had converted the people of the Madeira archipelago to Christianity! Henry, apparently, was confident that the pope would never know that the islands had no inhabitants at all.

As with the rest of his conquests, Henry never visited Madeira. He was a loner by choice, reserved in his manner and sometimes even described as melancholy. He always preferred to send others to search for foreign lands rather than explore them himself. But for the work he would later do, the work that would leave his mark on history, Henry would depend on the knowledge of others.

5

BEYOND THE POINT OF NO RETURN

I, Prester John, who reign supreme, exceed in riches, virtue and power all creatures who dwell under heaven . . . I am a devout Christian, and everywhere protect the Christians of our empire.
—Letter dated 1165, from fabled Christian leader
Prester John to Emperor Manuel Comnenus

With the Madeira colonization a success, Henry set his sights on other unexplored territories. Ship after ship left Lisbon, all with the single aim of traveling where none had been before—farther down the western coast of Africa— and into unexplored territory. Henry wanted to find trade routes that had nothing to do with Muslim middlemen. He wanted African goods, such as spices and cloth, to travel directly from African shores to Portugal, carried by Portuguese ships. According to the maps Henry had, there was a bit of land jutting from the Sahara desert called Cape Bojador (the "bulging" cape).

Prince Henry directed the first European exploration of Africa's west coast. This map from around 1500 was drawn by Juan de la Cosa with information gathered from Portuguese explorer Vasco da Gama's successful voyage around Africa to India from 1497 to 1498.

As seafaring tradition had it, any southern destination beyond the cape was impossible to navigate. It was said that no ships ever got around it and that any vessel that tried would sink in the process. Sailors, navigators, and cartographers alike believed that Cape Bojador was the farthest southern point on the western coast of Africa that was safe to sail, but Henry thought differently.

Though there is no record of the exact books and maps that Henry consulted about the western African coastline, it is likely that he believed these works were mostly fictional or inaccurate. Instead, he had faith in an account called the *Libro del Consçimiento del Mundo*, which told of a fourteenth-century Castilian's travels around the world. His journeys included more than one trip down Africa's western coast, farther south than Cape Bojador, to several African countries and ports. Leading historians of Henry's life believed it, too, and others were also strongly influenced by this information.

Henry, armed only with intuition and his belief in the fourteenth-century tale, felt that ships could get past Cape Bojador. He sent fifteen ships in the span of ten years, each failing to reach the cape. One ship, captained by Gil Eanes, finally made it there in 1434, proving Henry's intuition correct. The successful voyage did wonders for Henry's reputation, since, as the news of his "discovery" spread throughout Europe, he was considered by many to be one of the world's leading cartographers.

Prince Henry loved his new status as a successful mapmaker and made the most of it. His fame helped improve his reputation in Portugal, too, which had suffered, according to Zurara: "The longer it took for the enterprise [of exploration] to produce results, the more [the people's] criticisms grew. The worst of it was that not only plebeian [common] people but also those of higher rank spoke about the issue in a contemptuous way, believing that no profit would come from so much expense and effort."

Portuguese Shipbuilding

Successful exploration by the Portuguese was largely possible because of the ships they used. At the time of the voyage to Cape Bojador, the most popular ships were called barchas. These vessels were flat, like barges, with square sails. They also had oars, which meant that sailors spent much of their time and energy rowing over the ocean's waves. Henry knew that to go farther, he needed a faster boat. He decided to start using a ship called a caravel, which was used mostly for deep-sea fishing. The caravel's design differed from that of the barcha in two important ways. The first difference was its hull, which was flat. Its wooden boards were flush with each other, not overlapping. This made it much faster. The second design difference was in its triangular sails, which could catch

the wind much better than square sails, also increasing its speed. Alvise Ca' da Mosto, a Venetian explorer who spent several years with Henry in Portugal's court, wrote that the prince found great possibility in the caravels. "The caravels of Portugal, being the best ships that travel the seas under sail, he reckoned that, provided they were furnished with everything necessary, they could sail anywhere." After Prince Henry decided to use caravels, they became the chief method of travel for mariners during the age of exploration, which lasted for more than 200 years. They were among the ships used by Christopher Columbus and his crew to cross the Atlantic Ocean years later, in 1492.

Henry's plan was, just as the people of Portugal believed, one of considerable expense and effort. The small country had to furnish the ships and pay the crews. Each caravel needed about twenty men for the journey, plus supplies to sustain them. Henry tried to mix exploration with profit, too, by filling the caravels with soldiers who raided the Atlantic Coast from Morocco. Ca' da Mosto wrote of these raids in his book *Navigazioni*, "The said lord [Henry] strove by every possible means to do harm to this Kingdom of Fez. "

This engraving depicts a battle with native peoples in the early French and Portuguese colonization of what became known as Brazil. It was made in 1564 by the Dutch artist Theodor de Bry. The Portuguese explorer Pedro Álvares Cabral landed in Brazil and claimed it for Portugal while sailing to India in 1500.

The Portuguese Slave Trade

Henry did more than steal valuable goods from the native Africans; he stole Africa's people and made them into European slaves. After Portuguese ships reached Cape Bojador in 1434, Henry wanted to know as much as possible about this land that, up until then, no European had ever seen. Rather than spend extra money exploring the foreign land, Henry thought of a safer and less expensive idea. He ordered every ship from Portugal that discovered new land to return to Europe with one or two of its native people. Henry and his men could question them about their homeland after docking in Portugal. In this way, Henry helped to establish the European slave trade.

The Portuguese dreamt that much would come from their expense and effort. These dreams, in fact, were golden: In Henry's time, about two-thirds of the gold traded to Europe every year came by camel caravan across the Sahara desert from the western coast of Africa. The Europeans wanted to get the gold themselves and sail it back to the mainland without paying the Muslims.

Wealth interested Henry as well, since more gold would improve the status of Portugal. But crusading to spread Christianity was never far from Henry's mind. And, as his reputation

grew, so did his ego. The prince now saw himself as a leader of the Church and its main religious crusader. Under his leadership, Portuguese armies would forcibly spread the Catholic faith throughout the Muslim world.

Chasing a Legend

At the height of Prince Henry's notoriety and success, he was somewhat obsessed with a Christian hero, a man who was said to have ruled over Christian lands somewhere in the south or east. The legend of Prester John, the fabled Christian king of Africa, had been alive across the European continent for centuries. Its integrity was fueled by a letter addressed to Emperor Manuel Comnenus, Christian ruler of the Byzantine Empire, which told of the African king's desire to protect Christians from the powerful Muslim world.

As the legend went, Prester John had converted thousands of Ethiopians to Christianity. With them, he formed an army that was constantly warring with surrounding Muslims. It was said that he had his own Christian empire in eastern Africa. In an inscription on a map drawn in 1367, it was written that Prester's empire was so wealthy that the roofs of the houses there were made entirely of gold.

PRIESTER JOANNES.

This illustration of the fabled Prester John shows him dressed as an Asian king, complete with the symbols that Europeans associated with Asia: ornate turbans and sashes, obedient servants, and cowering subjects.

Henry had so much faith in finding Prester John's kingdom that he hoped to seal agreements with him that would form a vast trading network. In 1441, he instructed his explorers to find any news of the leader's fate and his empire. If the Portuguese could join forces with the king, then Africa—and all is riches—could be claimed by them. It was in this way that Henry believed he would reach the height of his fame. Prester John was Prince Henry's personal hero: He was a great leader and warrior, a man of terrific wealth and power, all while serving his faith.

Henry's ships and explorers had been successful on the western coast of Africa and had drawn maps of greater accuracy. They had returned with spices and other riches, and even native people that fortified the beginning of the Portuguese slave trade. Although Henry had grand dreams for himself and his legacy, he is remembered as "the Navigator." His voyages to the western coast of Africa cemented his name in history. By the middle of the fifteenth century, Henry still wanted to be a crusader, a process he felt had begun in Ceuta. This time, however, the Portuguese would sail hastily into the port city of Tangier.

6

TRAVESTY AT TANGIER

*And as [Prince Henry] proposed so he performed . . . despis–
ing all danger, and found the lands beyond quite contrary to
what he, like others, had expected. And although the matter
was a small one in itself, yet on account of its daring, was
reckoned great.*

—Gomes Eanes de Zurara, 1434, reprinted in
The Discoverers, Daniel J. Boorstin, 1983

It took Prince Henry the better part of the 1430s
to convince the royal court, including his own
family, to allow him to lead a crusade through
Africa. Henry's successful voyages along its western
coast did little to impress Portuguese leaders.
Sending individual ships to explore unknown territory was easy and inexpensive compared to launching a military campaign against an advanced
country such as Morocco. Any sort of crusade in
Africa would be costly and potentially disastrous.
The caution on the part of the Portuguese court
was wise.

Forms of warfare were changing rapidly toward the end of the Middle Ages. This illustration shows the sultan of Morocco watching as his army uses gunpowder to bombard a fortified town.

A Family Divided

Henry wanted to lead the invasion himself, but influential members of the royal court disagreed with both the idea of another crusade and Henry's leadership of it. Henry's younger brother, the Infante Don João, now old enough to consult his older brothers on matters of state, wrote an opinion paper in 1432. The paper, called a *parecer*, weighed the costs and benefits of Henry's plan. Though Henry's siblings and court officials wrote similar parecers, Don João's is the only one that survived. According to the paper, Henry was already lobbying for the grand crusade shortly after his first attack on Ceuta—even before finding any significant lands.

Portugal had no good reason to enter into any conflict with Morocco. The Muslim country posed no physical threat and had been a friendly trade partner. Morocco was not settled on any lands that once belonged to Christians that could thus be taken back. In addition, Don João argued, Christian law said that infidels must be converted by evangelism, not force, though in reality the crusaders seemed not to abide by this law.

Finally, Don João concluded that the most pressing argument against such a crusade was a financial one. The war would be too expensive for Portugal to absorb. It was a strain that the small country could little afford without

heavily taxing its people. As a general rule of chivalry, royalty was not supposed to burden its subjects too heavily. It would also be difficult in terms of manpower. If Portugal sent its army to fight in a foreign land, who would defend the country? The peace with Castile was delicate at best; the Iberian nation could always attack again. "It would be a bad joke if Portugal itself were lost to gain Asilah," Don João wrote. (Asilah was a small port city in Morocco.)

But the arguments in favor of such a crusade were also impressive. First, the Christian princes were duty-bound by God to spread their faith among the infidels. That mission could not be completed in Portugal. Moreover, conquering Morocco could help solve many of Portugal's financial troubles. The country was much larger, with more people who could be taxed. Many of Morocco's cities were wealthy, and that, too, looked inviting to the small European kingdom. In the end, Don João wrote that the arguments both for a conflict and against it were equal. He would leave the decision of waging a holy crusade against Islam and the people of Morocco to the king.

Sensing the king's hesitation, Henry offered him another option. He proposed taking a small force to Ceuta and launching attacks on Morocco from there. Even better still, Henry would finance this smaller expedition.

65

This is the royal tomb of King João I and Queen Philippa. It is located at the Batalha Monastery, in Batalha, Portugal.

Then another parecer appeared, this time written by the count of Ourém on June 4, 1432. He nixed Henry's new idea. Ourém wrote that everyone knew that the prince's household was smaller than he claimed, so he wouldn't even have the manpower to ensure Portugal's success. Henry also, like the rest of his brothers, didn't have great wealth. The king, Ourém said, would eventually have to send money, soldiers, and ships to save this force that was probably doomed to fail. He wrote harshly, "Since Prince Henry is such a greathearted man, he would not be content to remain in Ceuta without attempting great

feats of arms. The outcome of these expeditions would necessarily be doubtful because he would only dispose of such small forces to undertake them that, if things went awry (which God willing they should not) you would then be obliged to go to his rescue with all the forces you could raise."

But King João I never made any decision. He died in 1433. Arguments for or against the proposal no longer mattered. Any expeditions would have to be delayed.

The discussions about the expeditions to Morocco continued over the next several years. For the most part, opinion remained against Henry. Still, he never forgot his dream and constantly argued for the chance to lead the crusade. In response to the negative opinions that were circulating in his homeland, Henry wrote his own parecer in 1436, this time addressed to his brother, Duarte, the new king. Quoting the Bible and rejecting his detractors' arguments, he spoke in sweeping terms of destiny and duty. Even though he seemed to be the only person at court who thought a crusade in Morocco was a good idea, he managed to convince King Duarte. Henry got his army in 1436, a force of 14,000 men. He would be its commander, with his brother Pedro directly under him. Another younger brother, Fernando, accompanied Pedro and Henry on the voyage. His presence at the attack would prove fatal.

Mission to Morocco

What must have been a source of considerable pride for Henry was short-lived. The crusade, which seemed doomed from its very beginning, lacked ships. As with the invasion of Ceuta, Portugal had to obtain vessels from other countries. This took time and money, delaying the launch until August 22, 1437. But there was ongoing trouble. Portugal still lacked enough ships to transport its army, and Henry had to leave half of his men behind. For a battle that was already determined to be difficult at best, Henry's ships could transport only 7,000 of his soldiers. The prince's advisers suggested that, given the troop shortage, he await further instructions from the king. Henry would have none of it; in his mind, he had come too close to now waver. As a result, the crusade to convert Morocco's Muslims began on September 8, 1437, when Henry and his depleted army sailed to Tangier.

Unlike with Ceuta, it was no great secret this time that Portugal was going to attack Tangier. Henry found the Moroccan city had not only prepared to defend itself but was also secure in its ability to win a fight. Tangier was solidly enclosed by a wall, although Henry had told the king that the walls were weak and

falling apart. Moroccan soldiers were waiting for the prince's army in great numbers. There seemed to be no way to take the city other than by a direct assault. Perhaps the worst fact of all was that the governor of Tangier was ben Salah, the same man who had led and lost Ceuta to Henry in 1415.

In the days after the Portuguese army arrived at Tangier and built a stockade on the beach there, even more blunders were discovered. Henry had not brought sufficient artillery with him to do any damage to the city's fortifications. Even the ladders brought to scale the walls were useless—they were too short to reach the top. Although Henry had the army build another stockade outside the city, he made no proper haven from it to the sea. The beach was wide open, leaving the army's only potential escape route incredibly dangerous.

King Duarte had ordered Henry to make no more than three assaults and spend no more than a week in Tangier. If it took longer than that to conquer the city, Morocco would have plenty of time to call for reinforcements. As it stood, Henry would also have to return to Ceuta for the winter to gather more supplies. But with typical disregard for authority, Henry disobeyed the new king. He allowed the army to remain outside the city for five weeks.

Fighting with Dwindled Forces

With these obstacles, the prince's effectiveness as a leader quickly deteriorated. It was impossible for him to see that this crusade would be anything but a failure. Still, Henry stubbornly believed that God was protecting his fight. He firmly insisted that his army would capture the city simply because it was God's will. It is unlikely that his soldiers were so convinced. At least 1,000 of them fled the false safety of the stockade and ran for the ships after the first week of fighting. Two thousand more soldiers followed, leaving Henry with a force of only 4,000 men by early October.

His only option was withdrawal. The Moroccan army was growing stronger every day, making it impossible for the Portuguese to take the city. Under pressure from the military leaders, Henry looked for a solution. His only answer came immediately.

Although it was a bitter concession, he offered the Muslims their city of Ceuta. Not only had its capture twenty-two years earlier marked Henry's most famous success, but his father, King João I, had put him in charge of the city's defense.

After being repulsed by the Muslims in 1437, later kings of Portugal continued to try to gain a foothold in Morocco. This nineteenth-century illustration shows King Sebastian, who was encouraged by Jesuit priests to wage war in Africa, at the Battle of Alcazarquivir in Morocco, where he died in 1578.

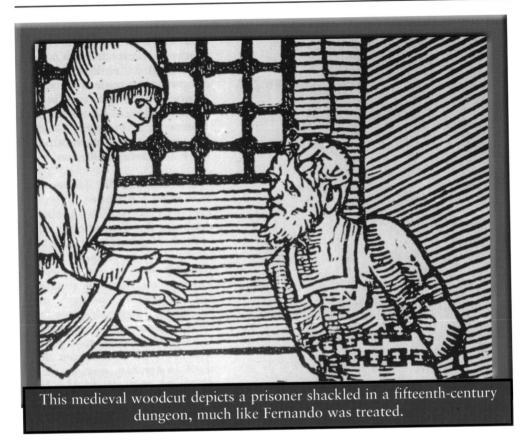

This medieval woodcut depicts a prisoner shackled in a fifteenth-century dungeon, much like Fernando was treated.

To surrender Ceuta now seemed a double humiliation, but by October 17, Henry and twelve others, including his brother Pedro, signed away possession of the city. The surrender agreement read, "For the sake of peace and concord I give my undertaking to you, ben Salah, that I shall hand over to you the city of Ceuta, together with all captive Moors who may be held there or those who are there as hostages for other captives; also those who are held aboard the fleet or the camp here. To guarantee that these things will be done I shall give you [as a hostage] the Prince D. Fernando, my brother."

But Prince Henry had no authority to surrender Ceuta. He also had no right to sacrifice his younger brother as a hostage. Henry was a royal embarrassment, and he knew it. He returned to Ceuta for eight months under the guise of transferring the city back to the Moors and insuring the safe return of his sibling. Meanwhile, King Duarte tried everything he could to stall the return of Ceuta and save Portugal from any more ridicule.

Luckily for Portugal, fate intervened. King Duarte, who had fallen ill upon hearing the news of the disaster at Tangier, died in August 1438. But the heir to the throne, Alfonso V, was only six years old. Henry's brother Pedro was appointed regent, or substitute monarch, until Alfonso came of age. At this point, Henry continued stalling the return of the island while Fernando's plight worsened. If he died, the return of Ceuta would be voided. Fernando's death was the perfect solution for Portugal. And when he died in 1443, in a Muslim dungeon after being tortured by the Moors, Henry had him depicted as a martyr.

7

SLAVES AND
CIVET CATS

For some [slaves] kept their heads low and their faces bathed in tears . . . and it was needful to part father from son, husbands from wives, brothers from brothers . . . each fell where his lot took him.
—Gomes Eanes de Zurara, 1441

With the Tangier debacle behind him, Henry returned to exploring and continued to send ships to the Saharan coast. There were two goals of these voyages, which were almost always in conflict with each other. For instance, the soldiers who set sail for Africa were, like Henry, interested in the glories gained by crusading. Their objective was to forcibly convert the Saharan natives from their Muslim faith to Christianity. But the merchants who funded these voyages were more interested in trading and increasing their profits. The conflict arose because people who were attacked were not very interested in trade negotiations.

The Sudan and other areas of the Arabian Peninsula were vital trade routes for Europeans and Muslims, who bartered a wide variety of goods, such as spices and grains, as pictured here.

The trading of goods is what, for a short time, prevented violence. Henry's men were still under orders to essentially attack any native people they found in the Sahara desert, but if a trade deal could be negotiated, the violence stopped.

The Silent Trade

Trading goods helped preserve the relationships between people. Investors were most pleased with precious metals such as gold, which was still the most sought-after material. The ships often returned with other items, too, such as gum arabic, a sticky substance from trees that was used as an adhesive, as well as ostrich eggs, camels, cattle, and goats. A civet cat, a type of wild cat, was also prized. It naturally produced a liquid called musk. In case no musk could be found, the cat itself would be loaded aboard the ship.

In exchange for these goods, the Portuguese offered the Muslims items that were rare in the Sahara desert. Wheat, for instance, was a leading export to Africa. The grain, though a staple, was scarce in the desert and it fetched a fine price. The Saharans had no interest in European clothing, however, as it was not suited for such hot weather. But the clothing worn by the Arabs in North Africa was perfect for Portugal's climate. Other woolen and linen textiles were also traded.

Trading caravans established relationships between people of distant lands. Portuguese traders sold items to the Muslims that were unavailable in the desert, while the Muslims brought spices and other goods that could not be found in Portugal.

Trading between people who did not speak the same language was difficult, however. The Moroccans, who would make their way across the desert to Europe with African goods, practiced what was known as silent trade, mostly with native people along the Senegal River, writes historian Daniel J. Boorstin. During these silent transactions, the Moroccans would lay out piles of salt, beads, and other goods unavailable in the region. Then they would hide and wait for the native people to come out with gold pieces.

Shortly before Prince Henry's death in 1460, the Venetian navigator Alvise Ca' da Mosto wrote of Portuguese holdings in Africa. "[The Portuguese] buy and sell with the Arabs who come to the coast to trade for merchandise of various kinds, such as woollen cloths, cotton, silver, and 'alchezeli,' that is, cloaks, carpets, and similar articles and above all, corn [wheat], for they are always short of food." This detail of a fifteenth-century African map depicts a trading fortress on the Gold Coast.

The native people would leave stacks of gold in various amounts next to the piles of Moroccan goods, thus indicating their value. Afterward, the native people would hide. Next, the Muslims would come and either take the gold or reduce the amount of items in the pile. This tedious practice was said to have fascinated Prince Henry. It made the prospect of trade, already a good idea for the country, an interesting project for the prince.

As Henry's men made their way farther south, peaceful trade was a much safer alternative to war. The Sahara was sparsely inhabited and tranquil. But as the caravels continued down the coast, deeper into what was then alternately called Guinea or "Black Africa" (distinguishing the region from that of the Arabs), danger grew.

While a ship full of soldiers could handle a small band of nomads, they were no challenge for an entire tribe. Nor were their weapons. The indigenous tribes had poisoned spears and arrows, which would kill the Portuguese quickly and painfully. The Africans did not always wait to be attacked either. Sometimes they would row out to the caravels in dugout canoes and surprise the Portuguese, who were still on board.

Henry's caravels continued on trade missions in the region throughout the 1440s. It was not until 1447 that the goal of Portuguese expeditions would dramatically change from one that existed primarily for the exchange of goods to one that was largely an ongoing slave trade.

The Burgeoning Slave Trade

For years, Henry had ordered his ships to return with one or two native people. In the beginning, it was apparently for the purpose of learning more about the land, but many of those kidnapped never saw their homeland again. As soon as Henry's men realized

that the sale of human beings was lucrative, the kidnapping of native people became more frequent. There is no record to indicate that Henry ever did anything to discourage this practice. Instead, he helped to motivate it.

While the voyage in 1447 was the first record of slave trading involving Prince Henry, the Portuguese system of recruiting slaves had begun in 1444. One of Henry's men, a royal tax collector named Lançorte da Ilha, along with a group of merchants, funded a fleet of six ships expressly to return with human slaves. Though Henry did not finance the journey, he did reap some of its benefits. The prince was entitled to one-fifth of whatever the ships brought back. Originally, this fifth, called a *quinto*, was considered war booty. As the slave trade developed, however, the quinto became more of a tax.

When the ships returned on August 6, 1444, a huge crowd gathered at the dock, including the prince, who attended the event on horseback. He picked his quinto of forty-six slaves, Zurara wrote, and "thought it expedient to separate fathers and sons, wives and husbands, brothers and sisters [as] he respected no family ties or bonds of friendships."

A prospective buyer examines a slave in a market in Marrakesh, Morocco, in this 1907 painting. The slave trade, always profitable, became even more lucrative after the European discovery and colonization of the Americas. This led to a triangular trade between Africa, Europe, and the New World. African slaves were brought to the New World as early as 1502.

The fleet's homecoming was considered a celebration of sorts. With so many slaves to be sold, Portugal had just established itself as a partner in the European slave trade. The small country was now just as important a trader as Italy or Spain, countries that also profited from the buying and selling of human beings.

While slaves were not as worthwhile as gold, they were certainly valuable. The return of Ilha's fleet meant that the money that had been invested over the years by Portuguese merchants had not been wasted. After years of searching foreign shores, all of this navigating would finally be profitable. Zurara wrote in his book *Chronicle of the Discovery and Conquest of Guinea*, "From thence onward, therefore, their enthusiasm grew more and more, seeing, as they did, the houses of others full of slaves, and their estates on the increase."

Profit from Bound Hands

Later, Henry would earn considerable profits as well. By December 26, 1457, he ordered a tax levied on all goods and slaves coming from Africa into Portugal. This tax was to be paid to Portugal's Order of Christ. And since he was the order's administrator, the money benefited him, too.

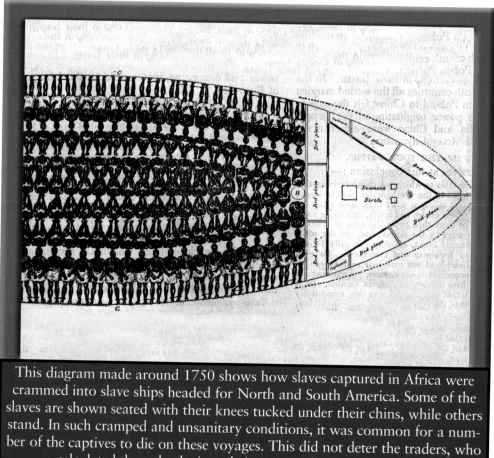

This diagram made around 1750 shows how slaves captured in Africa were crammed into slave ships headed for North and South America. Some of the slaves are shown seated with their knees tucked under their chins, while others stand. In such cramped and unsanitary conditions, it was common for a number of the captives to die on these voyages. This did not deter the traders, who calculated these deaths into their costs and still made a profit.

During the remainder of Henry's life, he spoke of converting the slaves to Catholicism. And Zurara, mindful of others' criticism, painted a noble picture of the prince having only the salvation of slaves in mind. However, considering the profit that Henry made from the slave trade, this is unlikely. Also, given the large number of slaves that were sold to owners outside of Portugal, there is little evidence that Henry had the

opportunity, even if he did have the conviction, to preach Christianity. Not only did he earn profits from trading slaves, but he bought and sold them himself. At the time of his death, he owned eight slaves.

While Prince Henry in no way started the slave trade, he was a major contributor to its growth. He helped Portugal become a major slave trading country that would maintain its power for hundreds of years afterward.

Although the Portuguese stopped shipping slaves north of the equator in 1816, they continued to send them to Brazil, which eventually became Portugal's largest colony and market for slave labor. The slave trade was a great source of pride for the Portuguese, too, as it put them in the same league with the Spanish and Italians, countries whose power had been established long before Portugal's.

And, through his advancements in navigation, Prince Henry demonstrated that he could transport slaves to Europe faster than ever before. Europeans would never again be forced to purchase slaves from Arabic traders who traveled on foot across the desert. Instead, ships could travel across the sea, kidnap the native people, and bring them back to Europe in weeks, not months. This process saved both time and money,

since there was no need to pay the Arab middle-men. In addition, more slaves could be crammed in the hold of a ship than could walk across the desert, causing a massive tide of slave labor into Europe. For hundreds of years after the death of Prince Henry, and mostly because of his contri-butions to navigation, slavery exploded from Europe to the Americas.

8

FINAL VOYAGES

Enough for us that the hidden half of the globe is brought to light, and the Portuguese daily go farther and farther beyond the equator. Thus shores unknown will soon become accessible; for one in emulation of another sets forth in labours and mighty perils.
—Peter Martyr, 1493, reprinted in *The Discoverers* by Daniel Boorstin, 1983

Prince Henry sponsored missions of exploration until his death in 1460, when he was still sending mariners to the Canary Islands. The embarrassing defeat of the Portuguese in the islands in 1424 did not stop his dreams of glory. By 1446, after numerous attempts to colonize the area, Henry attained control over all Portuguese ships sailing for the Canary Islands. The islands, known to be pagan, were prime prizes for the crusading prince, though his success there was limited.

After the failed 1424 attempt to settle the island group, Henry did not mount another large expedition until 1434. Which island the sailors attacked is unknown, but Henry's men again met with failure. In a report to Pope Eugenius IV,

Under Prince Henry, the sailing vessel known as the Portuguese caravel *(above)* was developed, techniques of cartography were advanced, navigational instruments were improved, and commerce by sea increased. He also designed a grand strategy to enable Christian Europe to overwhelm the power of Islam by establishing contact with Asia and Africa.

Henry said he had 400 converts—actually slaves—but his claim satisfied the crusading aspects of the voyage. As a military accomplishment, Henry's men failed again. The prince told the pope that the uncivilized native people of the island were incapable of fighting a traditional war. Instead of confronting the Portuguese face-to-face, the native people fiercely defended themselves from inside caves. The pope responded in 1436 by granting the Portuguese the sole right to conquer and rule any of the Canary Islands not already settled by Christians, which excluded several of the smaller islands. The pope changed his mind just three months later, for, according to Zurara's account, Portugal was not the only country interested in the Canary Islands; Spain had also tried to conquer them.

A Dream Postponed

With the defeat at Tangier and death of King Duarte in 1438, Henry was forced to abandon his dreams of colonizing the remaining Canary Islands. In his next attempt, the prince—in a manner that was uncharacteristic of him—completely lacked diplomacy.

Four different tribes lived on the island of La Gomera, and Henry, through a small Portuguese settlement on that island, became friendly with the tribes' chiefs. The chiefs, who were often at war with other tribes, were happy to help Henry's men capture slaves from other islands to be sold in Portugal.

ALPHONSVS V. LVSITANIÆ REX XII.
Eduardo uita functo Regnum recepit Alphonsus sex annos natus. Eius administrationem ab Eleonora matre susceptâ Lusitani Proceres Eduardi uoluntate posthabita ad Petrum eiusdem fratrê suâ deferunt Iste ea fidelitẽ perfunc.

Because Alfonso V was just six years of age when his father, Duarte, died, the question of regency led to an ugly battle between his uncle Pedro and his mother. Later on, Alfonso was swayed by the duke of Bragança, who was also João I's illegitimate son, into having Pedro killed.

In the 1440s and 1450s, Henry's rights to conquer the Canary Islands were constantly questioned. The Castilians continued to claim that the Canaries belonged to them and that they had been there first.

King João II, of Castile, frequently wrote to Alfonso V, criticizing Henry's constant attacks on the island of Lanzarote. Castile controlled Lanzarote, and João's men had been attacked several times by the Portuguese. By ordering the attacks on the Castilians, Prince Henry was essentially violating the peace treaty between the two countries. Still, neither King Alfonso nor his uncle, Prince Henry, seemed to care.

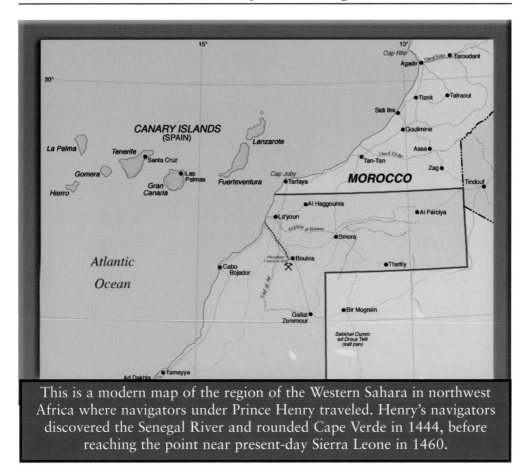

This is a modern map of the region of the Western Sahara in northwest Africa where navigators under Prince Henry traveled. Henry's navigators discovered the Senegal River and rounded Cape Verde in 1444, before reaching the point near present-day Sierra Leone in 1460.

In 1451, Henry again sent a fleet to Grand Canary Island. His men robbed and murdered not only islanders but also Spanish merchants from Andalusia, a region of Spain. Not surprisingly, tensions between the neighboring countries increased. And although war between Portugal and Castile seemed imminent, one important attempt at peace was about to take place. The heir to the Castilian throne, Enrique IV, was betrothed to Alfonso V's younger sister, Joana. The wedding, in 1455, was an important political union, and it

managed to calm hostilities between the two kingdoms. As Portugal had grown in wealth and importance, mostly thanks to Henry's exploration and slave trading, Castile retreated, breaking the peaceful alliance was not worth some small islands in the Atlantic Ocean. Henry, for his part, agreed to withdraw his men from the island, although he did not totally abandon sending ships to the region.

A New Challenge

The Canary Islands are a great example of Henry's stubbornness and determination. For decades, he spent large sums of money and lost many lives in his pursuit. Few people considered the island chain worth the effort he expended on it. In attempting to seize them, he gained neither fame nor glory, and increased his poor reputation as a misguided military leader.

Prince Henry would again be tested in such a role in Morocco. On September 30, 1458, he set sail for the Moroccan port of Alcácer-Ceguer, halfway between Tangier and Ceuta. The fleet, which numbered about ninety ships, found itself first at Tangier. King Alfonso, in a sudden rush for glory, changed his mind and decided the fleet would attack the city. Henry, perhaps in a desire not to repeat his previous defeat, talked Alfonso out of his desire to capture Tangier. The prince told the

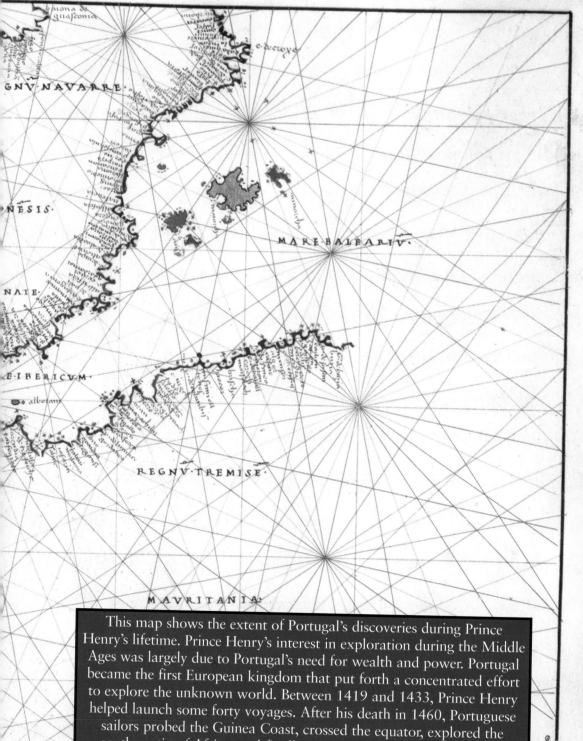

GNV·NAVARRE·

NESIS·

NATE·

E·IBERICVM·

alboran

MARE·BALBARIV·

REGNV·TREMISE·

MAVRITANIA

This map shows the extent of Portugal's discoveries during Prince Henry's lifetime. Prince Henry's interest in exploration during the Middle Ages was largely due to Portugal's need for wealth and power. Portugal became the first European kingdom that put forth a concentrated effort to explore the unknown world. Between 1419 and 1433, Prince Henry helped launch some forty voyages. After his death in 1460, Portuguese sailors probed the Guinea Coast, crossed the equator, explored the southern tip of Africa, and finally reached India in 1499. By 1542, Portuguese sailors had traveled all the way to Japan.

headstrong king that the soldiers were not psychologically prepared for such a battle and that going with the original plan, to conquer Alcácer-Ceguer, would surely be more successful. At Alcácer-Ceguer, Portuguese troops began attacking the city. When on the second night the battle seemed to pause, Henry suggested a bombardment. Cannons succeeded where armed soldiers failed, and the Portuguese entered the city as victors on October 24.

In these last few years before Henry's death, explorations in his name slowed. Henry's men were ordered to sail as far south as possible along the coast of western Africa before going inland along the Gambia River. A 1456 voyage led Henry's ships close to what is now Liberia. In the final voyage of what historians refer to as the age of Henrician discovery, a Portuguese knight named Pedro de Sintra made it to what is now Sierra Leone in 1461. Since Gil Eanes had rounded the elusive Cape Bojador in 1434, ships sent by Henry had traveled thousands of miles.

Prince Henry died of natural causes in 1460, but his work continued for years afterward. He helped usher in the age of discovery, which continued until 1520 and included Portugal's first expedition to India by Vasco da Gama, from

This monument of Prince Henry the Navigator, built in Lisbon in 1960, commemorates the 500th anniversary of his death.

1498 to 1499. However, instead of just hugging Africa's western coastline, as Henry's sailors had done, da Gama found a new sea route to India around the entire coast of Africa and across the Indian Ocean.

For a man who rarely left his library, and who was not known in his day for his own navigational prowess, Henry's reputation surpassed even his personal dreams of glory. History books do not call him Henry the Crusader or Henry the African Conqueror. Instead, he is known as Henry the Navigator, a prince who imagined a greater world than most people even thought existed. He believed that Portugal, once a small, impoverished kingdom, could be a world power known for its dramatic deeds throughout Europe and all of history.

CHRONOLOGY

1394 Prince Henry is born, the third son of King João I and Queen Philippa.

1408 Henry's father grants him his own land.

1415 A Portuguese fleet, with Henry on board, sets sail to conquer the Moroccan city of Ceuta. After the Portuguese are victorious, Henry is knighted.

1416 João I appoints Henry to be responsible for "all matters pertaining to our city of Ceuta and the defense thereof."

1420 Pope Martin V appoints Prince Henry administrator general of the Order of Christ.

1424 Henry sends a fleet to conquer the Canary Islands, but his army is defeated by native people.

1425 Portuguese settlers colonize the islands of Madeira and Porto Santo.

1432 Portuguese navigators discover the Azores.

1433 King João I dies, and his eldest son, Duarte, takes the throne.

1434 After fifteen failed expeditions, one of Prince Henry's ships rounds Africa's Cape Bojador, a fabled point of no return.

1434 to 1440s Prince Henry continues to send ships to the western coast of Africa, searching for gold and goods, and later slaves, as well as the legendary Prester John.

1437 Henry leads a fleet to capture Morocco's port city of Tangier. The disastrous expedition ultimately leads to the death six years later of Henry's younger brother Fernando, who was left as a hostage with the Moors.

1438 King Duarte dies, leaving the throne to his six-year-old son, Alfonso V. Henry's older brother, Pedro, is appointed regent.

1441 Prince Henry again takes up exploration of the Saharan coast and helps establish the Portuguese slave trade.

1444 The first ships carrying slaves for sale in Portugal arrive in Lagos from Africa.

1446 Henry receives control over all ships sailing from Portugal to the Canary Islands.

1458 Henry leads his last crusade, to Alcácer-Ceguer, a Moroccan port city. Unlike in Tangier, the Portuguese are victorious.

1460 Prince Henry dies at the age of sixty-six.

1461–1462 In the last of the Henrician voyages, ships make it as far south as present-day Sierra Leone.

1497–1498 Vasco da Gama reaches India via Africa's Cape of Good Hope.

GLOSSARY

benevolent   Expressing goodwill or kindly feelings.

burgeon   To grow or expand rapidly.

caravan   A group of people traveling together for safety.

cartographer   A mapmaker.

celibacy   Abstinence from sexual relations.

chivalry   The system, spirit, or customs practiced by medieval knights.

crusade   A military expedition undertaken in the name of Christ.

debacle   A disaster or fiasco.

delegate To grant responsibility to a deputy or a representative.

diplomacy The practice of conducting relationships between kingdoms or nations.

evangelism Preaching and spreading a belief, often in a zealous way.

exploitation The unjust and improper use of another person for profit.

fortified Having increased defenses.

illegitimate Born of parents who are not married to each other.

indigenous Originating in a particular environment.

inevitability Inability to be avoided.

Infante Title for a younger son of a Spanish or Portuguese monarch.

innovation The introduction of something new or different.

martyr   A person who sacrifices his or her life, usually for the principles of a religion.

melancholy   A depression of spirits.

naysayer   A person who disagrees.

pious   Showing devotion to religion and things divine.

plebeian   A commoner; of the common people.

portent   An omen or sign.

prophecy   The inspired declaration of divine will and purpose.

resin   A substance that comes from trees.

squires   Young men of noble birth who served knights.

staple   A main raw material or commodity, such as wheat, beef, or salt.

status   A person's place in society.

stipulate   To specify conditions of an agreement.

zealot   A fanatic, often of a religious nature.

FOR MORE
INFORMATION

The Mariners' Museum
100 Museum Drive
Newport News, VA 23606
(757) 596-2222
Web site: http://www.mariner.org

National Maritime Museum
Greenwich, London SE10 9NF
England
(44) 020 8858 4422
Web site: http://www.nmm.ac.uk

Portuguese Heritage Society of California
P.O. Box 18277
San Jose, CA 95158
Web site: http://www.serve.com/phsc/index.shtml

Web Sites

Due to the changing nature of Internet links, the Rosen Publishing Group, Inc., has developed an online list of Web sites related to the subject of this book. This site is updated regularly. Please use this link to access the list:

http://www.rosenlinks.com/lee/prhn/

FOR FURTHER READING

Corrick, James A. *The Early Middle Ages*. Chicago, IL: Gale-Lucent Books, 1994.

Fritz, Jean. *Around the World in a Hundred Years: From Henry the Navigator to Magellan*. New York: Penguin Putnam, 1994.

Hay, Jeff, ed. *The Middle Ages*. Chicago, IL: Gale-Lucent Books, 1994.

Matthews, Rupert. *Eyewitness: Explorer*. New York: DK Publishing, 2000.

McEvedy, Colin. *The New Penguin Atlas of Medieval History*. New York: Penguin USA, 1992.

Ross, Stewart. *Conquerors and Explorers*. Brookfield, CT: Copper Beech Books, 1996.

Stefoff, Rebecca. *Marco Polo and the Medieval Explorers*. New York: Chelsea House, 1990.

Stefoff, Rebecca. *Vasco da Gama and the Portuguese Explorers* (World Explorers). New York: Chelsea House, 1990.

Wilford, John Noble. *The Mapmakers*. New York: Knopf, 1981.

BIBLIOGRAPHY

Associação Nacional de Cruzeiros. "Ships of the Discoveries" (http://www.edinfor.pt/anc/ancr-bdesobertas-e.html). Retrieved December 2001.

Boorstin, Daniel. *The Discoverers: A History of Man's Search to Know His World and Himself.* New York: Random House, 1983.

The Mariners' Museum. "Maps and Charts of the Fifteenth Century." (http://www.mariner.org/age/maps.html). Retrieved December 2001.

Martins, J. P. Oliveira. *The Golden Age of Prince Henry the Navigator.* Safety Harbor, FL: Simon Publications, 2001.

Morison, Samuel Eliot. *The Great Explorers: The European Discovery of America.* New York: Oxford University Press, 1978.

Russell, Peter. *Prince Henry "the Navigator": A Life.*
London: Yale University Press, 2001.

Zurara, Gomes Eanes de. *The Chronicles of the
Discovery and Conquest of Guinea.* Edited and
translated by C. Raymond Beazley and Edgar
Prestage. London: Hakluyt Society, 1896.

INDEX

About the Author

Aileen Gallagher has written for several print and online publications, including the *New York Law Journal*, TheStreet.com, the *National Law Journal*, and Ironminds.com. This is her second book for Rosen Publishing; the first was a biography of Walter Payton. She lives and writes in New York City.

Photo Credits

Cover © Giraudon/Art Resource, NY; p. 4 © Wolfgang Kaehler/Corbis; pp. 7, 90 © maps.com/Corbis; pp. 11, 21, 30 © Bettmann/Corbis; pp. 13, 25, 56, 72 © Archivo Iconografico, S.A./Corbis; pp. 15, 18, 34, 40, 53, 77 © North Wind Picture Archives; p. 22 © Stapleton Collection/Corbis; pp. 27, 87 © Historical Picture Archives/Corbis; p. 33 © Araldo de Luca/Corbis; pp. 35, 46, 49, 83, 89 © Hulton/Archive/Getty Images; p. 43 © Art Resource; pp. 60, 63, 70, 75, 81 © Mary Evans Picture Library; p. 66 © Dave G. Houser/Corbis; p. 78 © The Granger Collection; pp. 92–93 © Corbis; p. 95 © Ric Ergenbright/Corbis.

Series Design

Tahara Hasan

Layout

Les Kanturek

Editor

Joann Jovinelly